AF381331

GUSTAV KLIMT

An icon of fin-de-siècle art

Written by Nadège Durant
In collaboration with Angélique Demur
Translated by Rebecca Neal

Art & Literature   50MINUTES.com

GUSTAV KLIMT

- **Born:** 14 July 1862 in Baumgarten (Austria).
- **Died:** 6 February 1918 in Vienna.
- **Context:** the Art Nouveau and Symbolist movements in Vienna at the turn of the 20th century.
- **Notable works:**
  - *Pallas Athene* (1898), painting
  - *Beethoven Frieze* (1902), painting
  - *Philosophy* (1907), painting
  - *The Kiss* (1907-1908), painting
  - *Danaë* (1907-1908), painting

Gustav Klimt was one of the leading members of the Vienna Secession, a movement closely associated with Art Nouveau that flourished in Vienna at the turn of the 20th century and revitalised Austrian art.

At the beginning of his career, Klimt was known for his neoclassical wall paintings, before turning away from the conventional style that had brought him success and recognition to become one of the founding members of the Vienna Secession. His vast body of work includes oil paintings, murals, sketches and objets d'art, as well as architectural decorations, cartoons for tapestries and mosaics, ceramic works and lithographs. His most frequent subject was the female body, which he depicted with frank eroticism, and he often incorporated sensual and exotic elements into his work. His output was modern and innovative, and featured a wide range of characters, allegorical subjects, nudes, portraits and landscapes.

However, even when the sexual symbolism and eroticism of his work were veiled by allegory, they proved too much for the Viennese middle classes. Klimt was at the forefront of modern Austrian art, but although his work was admired by a new generation of avant-garde artists, it shocked conservatives and inspired heated debate. In spite of this initial controversy, many of his works are now considered to be key land-marks in art history.

CONTEXT

VIENNA IN 1900

Klimt's work was shaped by the thriving metropolis where he lived, namely Vienna, which, along with Paris, Brussels and London, was one of the great European cities at the start of the 20th century. At this time, the capital of the Austro-Hungarian Empire was in the midst of a period of continual economic and demographic growth, spurred by urban expansion and immigration. By 1900, Vienna was home to two million people, and Austria-Hungary as a whole had 50 million inhabitants.

From 1848 to 1916, the country was ruled by Emperor Franz Joseph I (1830-1916), who modernised and centralised its administration in Vienna, ordered the destruction of the city's ramparts, reduced customs tariffs, unified the tax system, played a key role in the foundation of the University of Vienna and implemented a number of other policies that cemented the city's status as the country's economic, scientific and artistic centre.

This transformation went hand in hand with a profound shift in the composition and customs of Viennese society. Immigrants from all over the Empire and beyond flocked to this cosmopolitan metropolis, which became a melting pot of different religions and customs. This cultural mixing led to the emergence of new social classes, and the first trade unions and political parties appeared. Although he was opposed to universal suffrage on principle, Franz Joseph eventually granted it under pressure from his subjects. As the middle class expanded and became an essential part of the economy, the aristocracy and the monarchy found their power under threat.

THE DECLINING ROLE OF THE ACADEMY

These social changes influenced the style of Klimt, whose early work was largely conventional. His mentors, in particular the painters Ferdinand Laufberger (1829-1881) and Julius Victor Berger (1850-1902), instilled ideals of beauty dating from antiquity in him, and as a result he spent the first years of his career reproducing Greek and Roman models in accordance with neoclassical principles.

Neoclassicism

Neoclassism emerged in Europe in the second half of the 18th century as a result of classical antiquity's growing influence on art. Painters at this time were inspired by the harmony, balance and simplicity of the art of antiquity and sought to replicate Greek and Roman forms in their own work.

However, by the early 1890s Klimt had begun to reflect on the evolution of society and art. In 1897, he and a number of other artists, including the architects and decorative artists Josef Maria Olbrich (1867-1908) and Josef Hoffman (1870-1956), established the Vienna Secession, a movement which was associated with Art Nouveau and which revolutionised the city's artistic scene.

The group's primary aim was to promote young local or foreign artists working across a range of different styles by exhibiting their work. They also produced an official magazine called *Ver Sacrum* (Latin for "Sacred Spring", 1897-1903), whose title referred to the ancient rite of renewal and hinted at their academic background, which they now sought to leave behind. In the magazine's inaugural issue, the writer Hermann Bahr (1863-1934) defined the Vienna Secession's mission by explaining that they did not view their stance as an aesthetic combat between the ancients and the moderns, but rather as a confrontation between two states of mind. Specifically, they stood in opposition to those who only created work to make money and whom they believed had a vested interest in preventing true art from thriving.

As such, the artists of this movement believed that art was being corrupted by money and sought to fight back against this trend. They thought that once artists no longer had to worry about the demands of their patrons, they would be entirely free to make their own aesthetic choices.

Art Nouveau

Art Nouveau was a European and American artistic and architectural movement that flourished between 1890 and 1905. It is a total art style, meaning that it encompasses many art forms (painting, music, the decorative arts, architecture, etc.). In Britain, it was initially referred to as the Modern Style, while in Belgium is was sometimes referred to as the *Style nouille* ("noodle style") or *Style coup de fouet* ("whiplash style").

THE INFLUENCE OF PSYCHOANALYSIS

This was an extremely productive period for Klimt, whose work was shaped by a host of new influences: for example, he discovered gold-ground painting and the Paleochristian mosaics of Ravenna and Venice. He also drew inspiration from Egyptian, Assyrian-Babylonian, Byzantine and Japanese art, like the Symbolists and Impressionists before him.

Symbolism and Impressionism

Symbolism was a literary and artistic movement that first appeared in the 1880s. As the movement's name suggests, Symbolist painters believed that art should represent an emotion or idea rather than depicting the natural world in an almost scientific way, as realist artists aimed to do.

Impressionism was a major artistic movement which dates from the late 19th and early 20th centuries and particularly flourished in France. Impressionist paintings make use of visible brush strokes and vivid colours to give a general impression of a scene rather than a detailed rendering.

Klimt also developed an interest in the theme of Eros and Thanatos (the god of love and the personification of death, respectively), which became popular in the early 20th century after Sigmund Freud (Austrian psychoanalyst, 1856-1939) incorporated it into his theories on life instincts and death instincts. Indeed, a number of Klimt's subjects are inspired by the work of Freud, who is widely acknowledged as the father of psychoanalysis and who argued that individuals are governed by unconscious forces that they cannot control. In *The Interpretation of Dreams* (1900), he theorised that our sexuality is one of the main driving forces behind our actions and desires, a hypothesis which scandalised Austrian society at the time. Klimt's work, which often features androgynous nude women in suggestive poses, evokes unrepressed sexuality and hints at the latent neurosis identified by Freud. Klimt also refers to the cycles of life with his phantasmagorical depictions of pregnancy, childhood and old age which resist a single definitive interpretation. In this way, he was one of the leading figures of a generation that was striving for change at the turn of the 20th century.

BIOGRAPHY

CHILDHOOD AND EARLY YEARS

Gustav Klimt was born on 14 July 1862 in Baumgarten, just outside Vienna. He was the second of seven children, and his parents were Ernst Klimt (1832-1892), a gold engraver who was originally from Bohemia (modern-day Czech Republic), and Anna Finster (1836-1915), who was originally from Vienna. The family's three sons, Gustav, Ernst and Georg, all displayed signs of artistic talent at an early age, much to their father's delight, but spent their childhood in poverty due to the lack of employment opportunities available to immigrants at that time.

Klimt developed a passion for historical painting and enrolled at the Vienna Kunstgewerbeschule, a school of applied arts and crafts, in 1876 to study architectural painting. Unlike many of his contemporaries, he accepted the conservative artistic principles taught there. In 1877, his youngest brother Ernst (1864-1892), who wanted to become an engraver like their father, also joined the

Kunstgewerbeschule, and the two brothers and their new classmate Franz Matsch (1861-1942) soon began working together. In 1883, they completed their studies and began producing art in a shared workshop that they referred to as the "Company of Artists". Klimt began his career by painting frescoes for public buildings in the capital, which enabled him to earn a comfortable living.

In 1888, he was awarded the Golden Order of Merit by Franz Josef I for his work on the Burgtheater in Vienna, before travelling to Krakow, Trieste, Venice and Munich. On his return, he became a member of an artists' association in Vienna and was offered a professorship at the Academy of Fine Arts Vienna, although he never actually took the position. It was also during this period that he met his partner and muse, Emilie Flöge (1874-1952), who appeared in a number of his paintings. 1892 marked a turning point in his career, as his father and his brother and colleague Ernst died in quick succession. Ernst also left his widow and child in Klimt's care. These two tragedies had a lasting impact on his artistic vision, as his subsequent works were less conventional and more personal.

THE VIENNA SECESSION

In 1897, Klimt left the Viennese artists' association he was a member of and helped to found the Vienna Secession and its official magazine, *Ver Sacrum.* The Austrian government supported the group's efforts and granted them public land to build an exhibition hall. The building was constructed by the architect Josef Maria Olbrich and came to be seen as emblematic of the Vienna Secession. The movement also adopted Pallas Athene, the Greek goddess of just causes, wisdom and the arts as its symbol; Klimt's 1898 painting of this goddess is now one of his best-known works.

In 1894, the Ministry of Education commissioned Klimt to paint the ceiling of the Great Hall of the University of Vienna, and he exhibited a sketch of one of these paintings, titled *Philosophy*, at the Secession Building in 1900, along with a number of landscapes. However, although the painting was awarded a gold medal at the Paris World's Fair, it was deemed pornographic and caused a scandal in Vienna.

In 1902, Klimt completed his *Beethoven Frieze*, which was exhibited at the 14th exhibition of the Vienna Secessionists. Three years later, Klimt and a number of other artists left the Vienna Secession.

KLIMT'S GOLDEN YEARS

In the final phase of his career, Klimt met with both popular and critical success. He travelled to London, Florence and Brussels, where he and a number of other artists worked on the Stoclet Palace, a mansion owned by the wealthy industrialist and art collector Adolphe Stoclet (1871-1949) which at that time was one of the most renowned Art Nouveau buildings. It is a particularly good example of the concept of total art, as its architectural design is in perfect harmony with its interior and exterior decorations, furniture, gardens and everyday objects. The dining room is entirely covered with mosaics in marble, glass and semi-precious stones, produced by Leopold Forstner (1878-1936) based on Klimt's sketches (*The Expectation*, *The Embrace*, *Tree of Life*).

Between 1907 and 1909, Klimt continued to work on his paintings for the University of Vienna

(*Philosophy*, *Medicine* and *Jurisprudence*), which the university ultimately rejected because of their overt eroticism. However, the works were exhibited in Vienna and Berlin. It was during this period that Klimt painted his most famous works, including *The Kiss*, which was produced between 1907 and 1908. In 1911, his painting *Death and Life* was awarded first prize at the International Art Exhibition in Rome, and exhibitions of his work were later held in Munich, Budapest, Mannheim and Dresden. He was also named an honorary member of the Academy of Decorative Arts in Rome, although he was rejected for a position at the Ministry of Education on four occasions.

On 11 January 1918, Klimt suffered a stroke in his apartment in Vienna. He died on 6 February, leaving a number of works unfinished.

CHARACTERISTICS OF KLIMT'S WORK

FOUR MAIN INTERESTS

Looking at Klimt's body of work as a whole, we can identify four key themes: portraits of women, allegories, the artist's vision of humanity and landscapes. Only a few of his paintings feature different subjects, including *Portrait of Joseph Pembauer, the Pianist and Piano Teacher* (1890) and *Schubert at the Piano* (1899), which were produced when Klimt depended on commissions from wealthy individuals to make a living. Indeed, from the early 20th century onwards, he produced no more portraits of men. Some art historians have suggested that the men depicted in some of his paintings (such as *The Kiss*) are actually Klimt himself, but the artist always denied this, claiming that he was not interested in himself as a subject and preferred to focus his attentions on other people (Fliedl, 1990: 192).

A study of Klimt's paintings and sketches inevitably leads to the conclusion that his preferred subject was women, who are depicted either directly or in allegorical form in his work. In Klimt's allegorical representations, his female figures are linked to abstract ideas, and he uses idealised depictions of the female body to impart a symbolic, erotic charge that is absent from the convention styles he learnt about during his studies. In his work, women become femme fatales who have the power to save the tortured human race through art and love.

THE ROLE OF LIGHT

Klimt's early paintings stand out for their subject matter, style and stunning iconography. Over the years, his works became increasingly dense, with every inch of the canvas filled with arabesques, scrolls, mosaics or intricate decorative motifs. However, arguably the main reason for his success is his use of gold and silver leaf in his paintings, a technique he used for the first time in *Pallas Athene* (1898).

The popularity of Klimt's "golden" works stems from their aesthetic beauty, gold's evocation of the material value of precious objects and the way that the gold creates a light effect that is in perfect harmony with the paintings' content. The richness of the gold recalls the frames of Byzantine and Russian religious icons, which draws a provocative connection between the sacred and the profane in Klimt's female nudes.

KLIMT AND THE ART OF SIMPLICITY

Klimt preferred to work from home, where he had a workshop, in comfortable clothing (sandals and a long robe with nothing underneath). He led a simple, almost reclusive life and devoted himself to his art and his family. Although Vienna's cafés were very popular with the city's intellectuals, he only rarely visited them, and he did not spend much time with other artists. Indeed, his reputation was such that he could afford to be selective in his choice of clients.

His approach to painting was very time-consuming, and his models often had to pose for long periods of time in his workshop. There were rumours that Klimt had relationships with his muses, possibly fuelled by the erotic nature of much of his work. Although he fathered 14 illegitimate children, he managed to keep his private life mostly secret and avoid any major scandals.

NOTABLE WORKS

PALLAS ATHENE

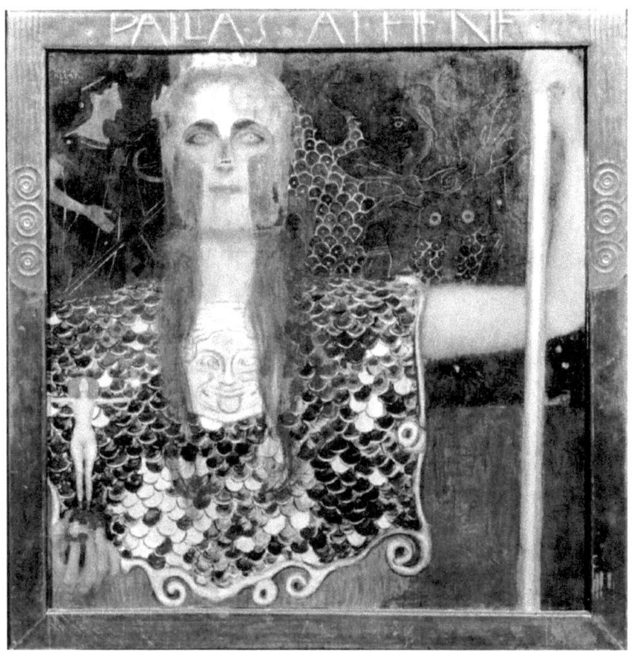

| Pallas Athene, 1898, oil painting on canvas, 75 x 75 cm, Vienna, Vienna Museum.

This work can be seen as the first step in Klimt's move away from conventional art. It was chosen as the poster for the first exhibition of the Vienna Secession in 1898.

As its title indicates, the painting represents the Greek goddess Athena, who is sometimes known as Pallas Athene after the giant Pallas, whom she flayed so that she could use his skin as a shield. In mythology, she is the goddess of wisdom, war and art and a somewhat androgynous figure.

Pallas Athene is a very different figure from Klimt's usual femme fatales. He is less concerned with depicting her femininity than the power and divinity she represents, and she is arguably the most powerful woman depicted in his body of work. It is nonetheless worth noting that sexual desire is linked to power in a number of his other paintings.

She is depicted wearing a helmet and armour, and is holding a *Nudas Veritas* ("nude truth") in one hand and a lance, the top and bottom of which are not visible, in the other. Klimt drew inspiration from numerous classical representations of Athene, but his work differs from them because he depicts the Gorgon (a mythological monster from antiquity which has snakes for hair) with its tongue sticking out on the goddess's armour. Furthermore, the use of gold leaf represents a break from tradition and gives Athene an archaic yet timeless dimension as a symbol of dreams and power.

BEETHOVEN FRIEZE

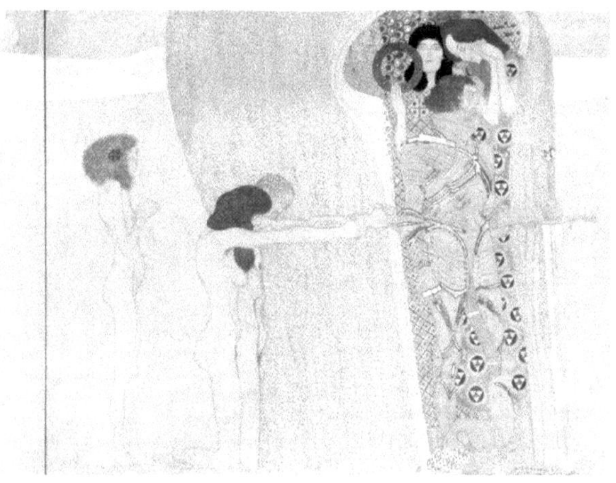

| *Beethoven Frieze*, 1902, casein paint on stucco, 220 x 1378 cm, Vienna, Österreichische Galerie Belvedere. Left-hand panel, *The Longing for Happiness*.

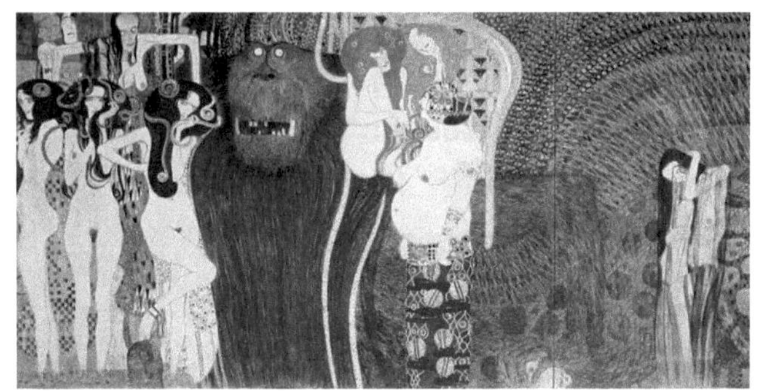

| Central panel, *Hostile Forces*.

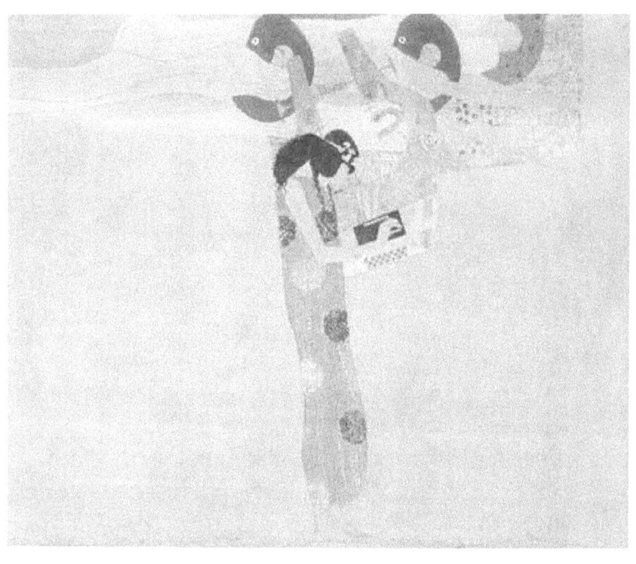

| First part of the right-hand panel, *The Kiss to the Whole World*.

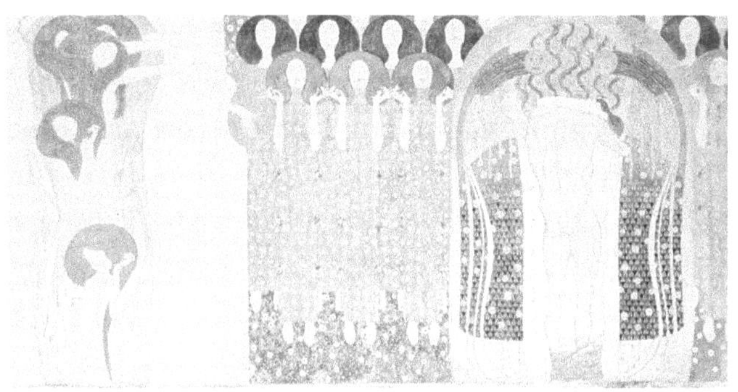

| Second part of the right-hand panel, *The Kiss to the Whole World*.

Klimt painted the *Beethoven Frieze* in 1902 for the 14th exhibition of the Vienna Secessionists, which was dedicated to the famous composer (1770-1827). It was painted directly onto the walls of the Secession Building using light materials, as Klimt was more concerned about his work's aesthetic value than its durability. Fortunately, the painting was preserved after the exhibition was over: in 1903, it was acquired by a collector, who detached it from the wall in seven pieces to move it. In 1973, the work was purchased by the Austrian government and restored. It was placed on display in a dedicated room in the Secession Building in 1986.

The frieze's central subject is the final chorus of Beethoven's *Ninth Symphony*, which represents the liberation of humanity through art and love. Like in a medieval tapestry, the work tells the story of this piece of music in a visual, linear form, so the viewer can follow it by "reading" from left to right.

The frieze is divided into three sections representing three very different scenes; their unifying thread is the fact that they each correspond to a feeling evoked by the *Ninth Symphony*. As a whole, the work illustrates humans' desire for happiness in a world of suffering caused by both external evil and inner weakness.

- The left panel, *The Longing for Happiness*, is almost 14 metres long and depicts "floating genies" which symbolise this desire, as well as three naked figures (a kneeling couple and a young girl standing behind them) who represent weak, suffering humanity. They are praying to three allegorical figures which Klimt labels "the Invisible Warrior", "Pity" and "Bravery", and which are larger than the praying people and sumptuously adorned with gold leaf.

- As its title (*Hostile Forces*) suggests, the central panel, which is 6.3 metres long, depicts evil powers working to thwart humans' hopes of happiness. On the left are three Gorgons, which take the form of naked women with long black hair and golden spirals representing the snakes, as well as three seemingly masked figures "Illness, Madness, Death" in the background. A significant proportion of the panel is occupied by Typhon, the father of the Gorgons, with vast blue wings. In the centre of the panel, we find "Sensuality, Lust and Intemperance", while on the right the image of a stooping, apparently suffering woman represents grief and pain.
- Finally, the right panel, *The Kiss to the Whole World*, features "poetry", represented by a female lute player, "the muses", who are opening the door to a world of happiness and love, and a choir of angels surrounding the "kiss to the entire world".

To produce this monumental work, Klimt used an array of different materials, some of which were unconventional: casein paint, stucco coating, gilt, pieces of mirrors, fragments of frosted glass, etc.

PHILOSOPHY

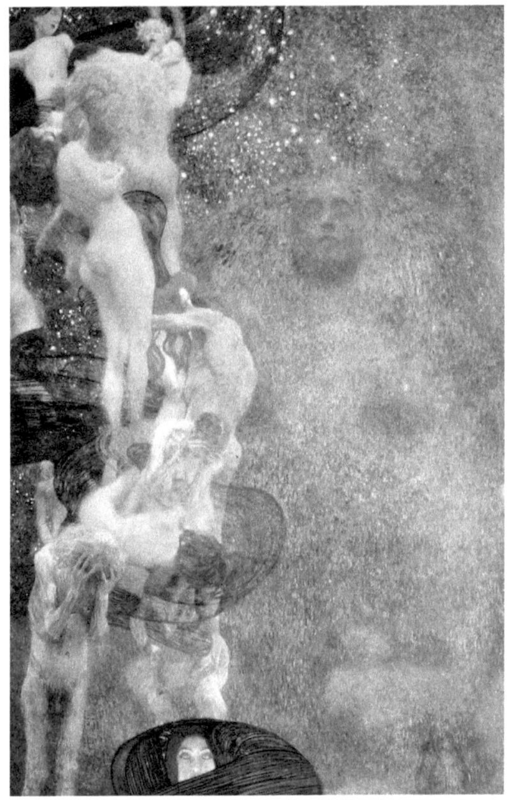

| *Philosophy*, oil painting on canvas, 430 x 300 cm, destroyed in a fire started by German troops as they retreated from Schloss Immendorf in Austria in 1945.

Philosophy is one of the three *Klimt University of Vienna Ceiling Paintings*, also known as the *Faculty Paintings*. As their name suggests, they were painted for the ceiling of the Great Hall of the University of Vienna between 1900 and 1907.

The sketch for *Philosophy* was displayed at the seventh exhibition of the Vienna Secessionists in March 1900, making it the first of the three works to be presented to the Austrian government. Although it was awarded a gold medal at the Paris World's Fair, the reception in Klimt's home country was far less positive, as critics focused their attention on the naked men and women who seem to be drifting in a kind of trance on the left-hand side of the painting. The painting's theme was initially supposed to be the triumph of light over darkness, but instead Klimt's work depicts an abstract, dreamlike mass which is accompanied by a bleak, almost empty space. Although this certainly represented a departure from traditional artwork, it was perfectly in tune with the atmosphere in Vienna at that time, which has been described as a "joyous apocalypse" (Clair, 1986).

After his work met with hostility and the three paintings were rejected by the University of

Vienna, Klimt decided to cancel his commission and return the advance he had been paid by the Austrian government. The works were then bought by the painter Koloman Moser (1868-1918) and the collector Erich Loderer. *Medicine* was subsequently displayed in an Austrian gallery, while *Philosophy* and *Jurisprudence* were acquired by Baron Bachofen-Echt, before being requisitioned by the government in 1938 because they belonged to a Jew. In May 1945, all three paintings were destroyed when retreating SS soldiers set fire to Schloss Immendorf to prevent any of the artworks there from falling into enemy hands. All that remains of them today is the initial sketches and a few photographs.

THE KISS

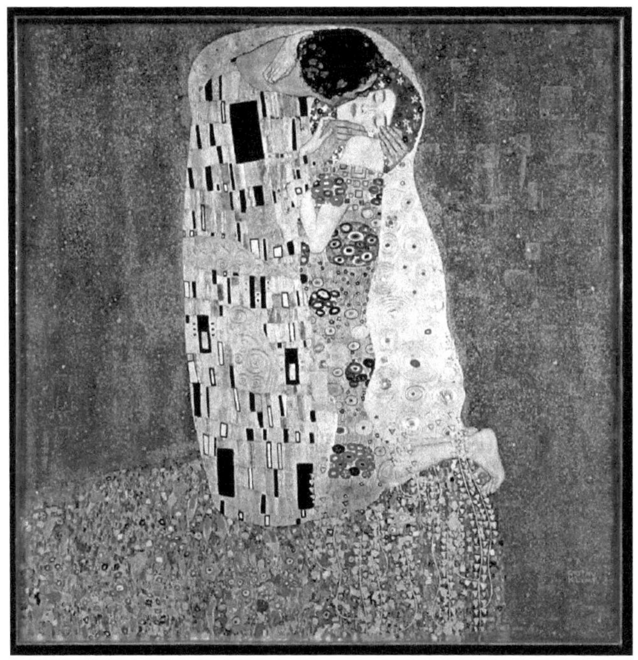

| *The Kiss*, 1907-1908, oil and gold painting on canvas, 180 x 180 cm, Vienna, Österreichische Galerie Belvedere.

The Kiss, which was produced between 1907 and 1908, is now considered an artistic masterpiece. It is one of the emblematic works of the Viennese Art Nouveau movement and Klimt's most popular painting, as proven by the countless reproductions of it.

The painting's success is largely down to two factors: the beauty of the gold used to create it and the sensual representation of happiness provided by the couple at its heart. It evokes a harmonious world in which the lovers, who are surrounded by a kind of golden halo, are so consumed by their love for one another that the world around them ceases to matter. The background and the carpet of flowers beneath their feet are similarly unimportant, and make it seem as though they are in their own bubble of time and space rather than a concrete location.

The canvas itself is a perfect square, and the painting depicts a couple embracing while dressed in clothes covered with complex motifs that form a kind of mosaic. The man is covered with black and white rectangles, while the woman wears coloured circles and flowers. The lovers are in an intimate pose: their faces are pressed together and their hands are intertwined. The woman is kneeling down with her eyes closed and seems to be giving herself up to her lover and allowing herself to be swept away by their shared passion.

From a technical point of view, the work combines traditional oil paint and gold leaf, which is typical of Klimt's so-called "golden phase".

DANAË

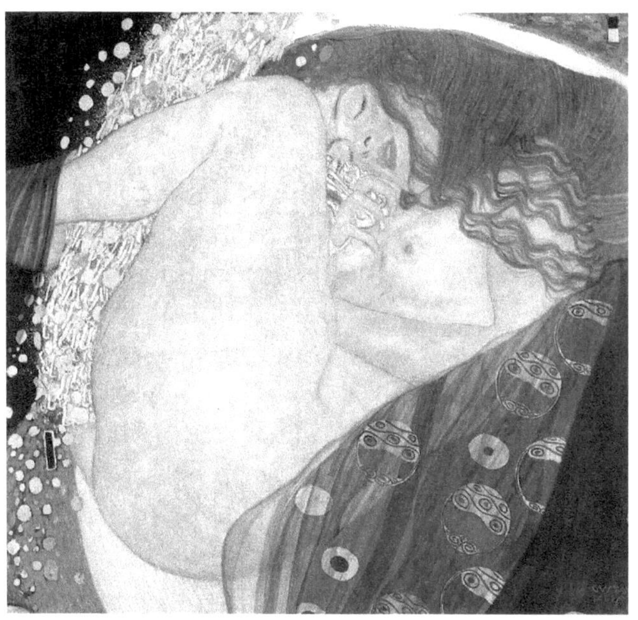

| *Danaë*, 1907-1908, oil painting on canvas, 77 x 83 cm, Graz, private collection.

This painting is based on the myth of Danaë. When the Oracle prophesied that Acrisius, king of Argos, would be murdered by his own grandson, he decided to imprison his daughter in a darkened tower where she would be sheltered from any temptation. However, the young woman caught the attention of Zeus, who impregnated her by assuming the form of golden rain. Klimt's painting is therefore a representation of procreation, as well as fertility and unabashed sexuality.

The distorted perspective of the painting serves to sexualise the young woman's entire body. Her thighs and buttocks are in the foreground, which places the viewer in a very intimate position in relation to her. Klimt's choice of colours makes Danaë's sexuality the main subject of the painting: her pale body is illuminated by gold and contrasts sharply with the black background. The close-up framing serves to emphasise her sexuality, while Zeus is relegated to a secondary position.

KLIMT'S LEGACY

Klimt's artistic influence is most evident in Vienna and Austria. His work inspired subsequent Viennese artists, including Egon Schiele (1890-1918), whose is best-known for his unconventional depictions of landscapes and the human body, and the painter and architect Friedensreich Hundertwasser (1928-2000), who was active decades later but who drew a great deal of inspiration from the revolution instigated by Klimt.

EGON SCHIELE

The Austrian painter Egon Schiele discovered the art of the Secessionists in Vienna. He met Klimt in 1907, when he was just 17 years old, and viewed him as a model and mentor. This admiration was reciprocated by the older artist. Although the two men differed in their style and the way they depicted their subjects, there are numerous similarities in their work.

From a stylistic point of view, both men were interested in the aesthetic of eroticism, but while Klimt's paintings are formally ordered and decorative, Schiele's are more tortured and expressive. In this sense, Klimt is more similar to the Dutch painter Piet Mondrian (1872-1944), in that he attempted to impose an overall order through formal means, while Schiele has more in common with the German painter Paul Klee (1879-1940), as he produced very personal works which also had the power to evoke shared experiences. While Klimt's work is considered emblematic of the fin-de-siècle aesthetic, Schiele's work is more in line with the ideas of the 20th century; together, they illustrate the incredible richness of art in the 1900s.

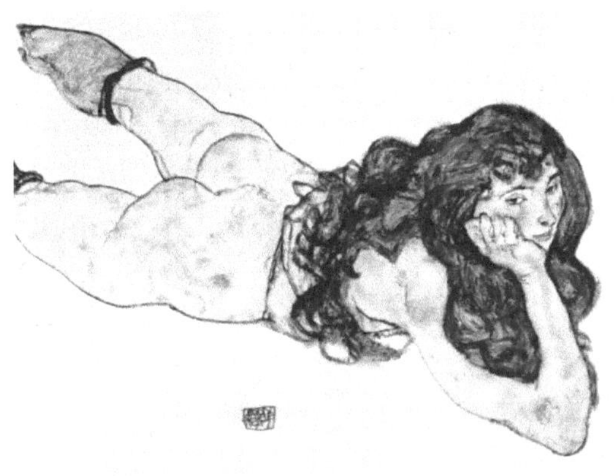

| Schiele, Egon, *Female Nude Lying on Her Stomach*, 1917, pencil and gouache on paper, 31 x 48 cm, private collection.

FRIEDENSREICH HUNDERTWASSER

Friedensreich Hundertwasser drew his inspiration from art, ecology and philosophy, and used vivid colours and organic forms to convey a strong sense of individualism and the reconciliation of humankind and nature. He rejected straight lines and was fascinated by spirals, and his use of organic forms and mosaics in his architectural work has inspired comparisons with Antoni Gaudí (Spanish architect, 1852-1926). His pictorial work is directly inspired by the art of the Vienna Secessionists, particularly Klimt and Schiele (although he never met either of them). As a whole, Hundertwasser's work symbolises Viennese art's shift towards Surrealism.

SURREALISM

Surrealism was a European artistic movement that flourished in the early 20th century. The movement's artists used methods based on mental processes such as automatism, dreams and the subconscious that were outside the power of reason and aimed to challenge accepted ideas. Surrealism therefore stood in opposition to naturalism and realism, which aimed to depict reality as faithfully as possible, without idealising or refining it.

SUMMARY

- Gustav Klimt was active during the transition between the 19th and 20th centuries. He spent his entire life in Vienna, which at that time was a thriving city and which had a major influence on his work. The Art Nouveau movement which was emerging in Europe at this time was inspired by both social change and a strong desire for artistic renewal.

- Klimt was the son of a Bohemian immigrant who worked as a gold engraver. He later enrolled at the Vienna Kunstgewerbeschule, where he received a conservative artistic education. During and after his studies, he produced neoclassical works on commission, alongside his brother Ernst and other artists.

- His brother's untimely death had a major impact on his work, and in 1897 he helped to found the Vienna Secession. This movement was closely associated with Art Nouveau and revolutionised art in Austria.

- Most of Klimt's works depict sensual female figures, allegories or landscapes, and his original choice of subjects was complemented by innovative artistic techniques. In particular, his success can be largely attributed to his style and his use of gold and silver in his paintings.

- In 1900, Klimt produced his sketch of *Philosophy* on commission from the Ministry of Education. The work's depiction of numerous erotic female allegorical figures caused a scandal in Vienna, although it was awarded a gold medal at the Paris World's Fair.
- In 1902, Klimt completed his *Beethoven Frieze*, which was painted on the walls of the Secession Building for the Vienna Secessionists' 14th exhibition. Its subject is the final chorus of the composer's *Ninth Symphony*, which evokes the liberation of humanity through art and love.
- Between 1907 and 1909, Klimt produced his most famous paintings, including *The Kiss* (1907-1908), which is now widely considered to be an artistic masterpiece. By this point, he was famous around the world and his work was exhibited in numerous different cities. He was viewed as the embodiment of the desire for change that permeated early 20th-century society.

FURTHER READING

BIBLIOGRAPHY

- Armiraglio, F. (2009) *Klimt*. Milan: Skira Mini Art Books.

- Baümer, A. (1986) *Gustav Klimt: Women*. London: Weidenfeld & Nicolson.

- Clair, J. (1986) *Vienne 1880-1938 : l'apocalypse joyeuse*. Paris: Centre Georges Pompidou.

- Fliedl, G. (1998) *Gustav Klimt: The World in Female Form*. Ann Arbor: Borders Press.

- Gaultier, A. (2005) *L'ABCdaire de Klimt*. Paris: Flammarion.

- Metzger, R. (2005) *Gustav Klimt: Drawings and Watercolors*. London: Thames & Hudson.

- Pabst, M. (1984) *L'Art graphique à Vienne autour de 1900*. Paris: Mercure de France.

FILMS AND DOCUMENTARIES

- *Klimt*. (2006) [Film]. Raoul Ruiz. Dir. Austria/France/Germany/UK: Epo-Film, Film-Line Productions GmbH, Lunar Films, Gémini Films.

ICONOGRAPHIC SOURCES

- *Lady with Fan*, 1917-1918, oil painting on canvas, 100 x 100 cm, Vienna, Leopold Museum. Royalty-free reproduction picture.

- *Pallas Athene*, 1898, oil painting on canvas, 75 x 75 cm, Vienna, Vienna Museum. Royalty-free reproduction picture.

- *Beethoven Frieze*, 1902, casein paint on stucco, 220 x 1378 cm, Vienna, Österreichische Galerie Belvedere. Royalty-free reproduction picture.

- *Philosophy*, oil painting on canvas, 430 x 300 cm, destroyed in a fire started by German troops as they retreated from Schloss Immendorf in Austria in 1945. Royalty-free reproduction picture.

- *The Kiss*, 1907-1908, oil and gold painting on canvas, 180 x 180 cm, Vienna, Österreichische Galerie Belvedere. Royalty-free reproduction picture.

- *Danaë*, 1907-1908, oil painting on canvas, 77 x 83 cm, Graz, private collection. Royalty-free reproduction picture.

- Schiele, Egon, *Female Nude Lying on Her Stomach*, 1917, pencil and gouache on paper, 31 x 48 cm, private collection. Royalty-free reproduction picture.

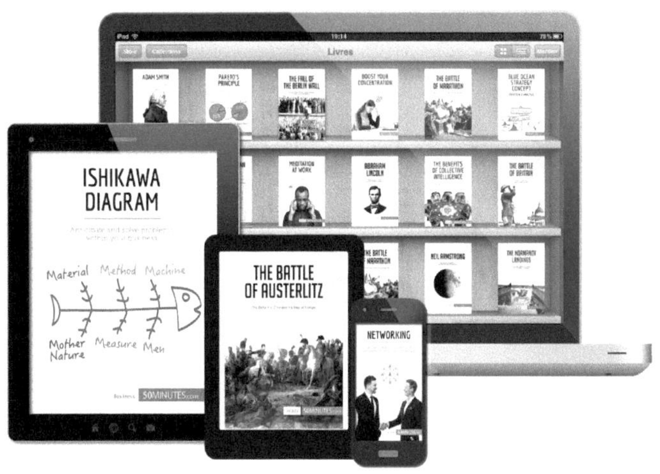

50MINUTES.com

IMPROVE YOUR GENERAL KNOWLEDGE
IN A BLINK OF AN EYE !

www.50minutes.com